안녕? 한글!

ANNYEONG? HANGEUL!

First published in 2024 by Hello Korean Inc.
© 2024 Prof. Jieun Kiaer with Derek Driggs and Hyung-Suk Kim

Published by Hur. Dae woo
Marketing by Kim. Cheol kyu / Hwang. Hyun kyung
Designed by Brunch Park
Cover Image by Lee. Seung mi
Character Design by Lee. Jae yeop
Special Support by Lee. Jong in (Boromwat, Jeju)

ISBN 979-11-988638-4-3 13700

Printed and bound in Republic of Korea by Hello Printec

ANNYEONG? HANGEUL!

안녕? 한글!

Prof. Jieun Kiaer

with Derek Driggs and Hyung-Suk Kim

Hello Korean

Welcome to learning Hangeul, the Korean alphabet! This book is for anyone who loves K-pop, K-dramas, Korean food, or wants to travel to Korea. It's also perfect if you just want to study the Korean alphabet. We hope you enjoy discovering how to read and write Hangeul with fun activities and interesting words.

We aim to make learning Hangeul enjoyable and accessible, even if you're a complete beginner. Through this book, you'll not only learn to read and write Hangeul but also discover many interesting Korean words and phrases.

Each chapter is packed with K-culture words to enhance your learning experience. Plus, every page features a QR code that links to audio instructions in multiple languages, including Indonesian, Chinese, Japanese, French, and, of course, Korean (more languages will be added). These recordings will guide you through the pronunciation of Korean words from left to right and top to bottom, with numbered guides for ease of use. This unique book allows friends from around the world to learn the Korean alphabet in their own languages. So, are you ready to start this exciting journey? Let's dive in and explore the beautiful world of Hangeul together!

한글(Korean alphabet)을 배우는 여정에 오신 것을 환영합니다! 이 책은 K-팝, K-드라마, 한국 음식을 사랑하거나 한국 여행을 계획 중인 분들을 위해 만들어졌습니다. 또는 단순히 한글을 배우고 싶으신 분들에게도 완벽한 선택입니다. 즐겁고 유익한 활동과 흥미로운 단어들을 통해 한글 읽기와 쓰기를 배우는 즐거움을 느끼시길 바랍니다.

이 책은 한글 학습을 처음 시작하는 분들도 쉽게 접근할 수 있도록 즐겁고 이해하기 쉬운 방식으로 구성되어 있습니다. 책을 통해 한글을 읽고 쓰는 법을 배우는 것은 물론, 흥미로운 한국어 단어와 문구들도 함께 발견하게 될 것입니다. 각 장에는 K-컬처 관련 단어들이 풍부하게 담겨 있어 학습 경험을 더욱 풍성하게 만들어 줍니다.

또한, 책의 모든 페이지에는 QR 코드가 포함되어 있어 인도네시아어, 중국어, 일본어, 프랑스어, 그리고 물론 한국어를 포함한 다양한 언어로 제공되는 음성 가이드로 연결됩니다(추가 언어는 계속 업데이트될 예정입니다). 이 음성 가이드는 한국어 단어의 발음을 왼쪽에서 오른쪽, 위에서 아래로 순서에 따라 쉽게 따라 할 수 있도록 번호와 함께 안내합니다. 이 독특한 책은 전 세계의 친구들이 각자의 언어로 한글을 배울 수 있는 기회를 제공합니다.
자, 이 흥미로운 여정을 시작할 준비가 되셨나요?
함께 아름다운 한글의 세계로 떠나봅시다!

About Us

This book is part of the *Annyeong? Korean! Textbook* series, which aims to spread the Korean language worldwide in many languages, not just English. For the first time, we are providing instructions in multiple languages to reach learners all around the globe. In this series, we have characters who are learning Korean. Let us introduce them to you!

이 책은 전 세계에 한국어를 전파하기 위해 만들어진 '안녕? 코리안!' 교재 시리즈의 일부로, 영어뿐만 아니라 여러 언어로 제공됩니다. 처음으로 다양한 언어로 학습 지침을 제공하여 전 세계 학습자들에게 다가가고자 합니다. 이 시리즈에는 한국어를 배우고 있는 캐릭터들이 등장합니다. 여러분께 이 책에 등장하는 캐릭터들을 소개해 드리겠습니다!

Sarang

Sarang has British-Korean background, and she is the manager of Sumbisori`s guest house, located near Hongdae station. She also works part-time at a convenience store.

사랑이는 영국-한국 혼혈 배경을 가지고 있으며, 홍대역 근처에 위치한 숨비소리 게스트하우스의 매니저입니다. 또한, 편의점에서 아르바이트를 하고 있습니다.

Priya

Priya is from Indonesia. In her country, she works in a company. She is in Korea because she is interested in Korean culture.

프리야는 인도네시아 출신입니다. 그녀는 자국에서 한 회사에 근무하고 있으며, 한국 문화에 관심이 있어 한국에 머물고 있습니다.

Haru

Haru is a Japanese student interested in Korean dramas and K-pop. He is in Seoul to learn Korean.

하루는 일본인 학생으로, 한국 드라마와 K-팝에 관심이 많습니다. 그는 한국어를 배우기 위해 서울에 머물고 있습니다.

Professor Caroline,

Caroline is from the US. She is professor of history at University, and she is in Korea to learn more about Korean culture and history.

캐롤라인은 미국 출신으로, 대학교에서 역사학 교수로 일하고 있습니다. 그녀는 한국 문화와 역사를 더 깊이 배우기 위해 한국에 머물고 있습니다.

Jina Ssaem

Jina Ssaem is a Korean teacher in Annyeong Korean Series

지나쌤은 안녕? 코리안! 시리즈에서 한국어를 가르치는 선생님입니다.

Sophia

Sophia is from France. She is passionate about sport, and she likes go hiking on Korean mountains.

소피아는 프랑스 출신으로, 스포츠에 열정적이며 한국의 산을 등산하는 것을 좋아합니다.

Yu Tao

Tao is from China. He likes Korean food and he is into e-sports.

타오는 중국 출신으로, 한국 음식을 좋아하며 e스포츠에 관심이 많습니다.

Sam

Sam is from Australia. He loves cooking and loves Australian football and baseball.

샘은 호주 출신으로, 요리를 좋아하며 호주 풋볼과 야구를 사랑합니다.

Gabriel ○────────────────────────────────────

Gabriel is from Canada. He studies architecture, and he is interested in Korean traditional houses. His grand-father participated in the Korean War.

가브리엘은 캐나다 출신으로 건축학을 전공하고 있으며, 한국의 전통 가옥에 관심이 많습니다. 그의 할아버지는 한국전쟁에 참전한 경험이 있습니다.

CHARACTER INTRODUCTIONS

Sumbisori`s guest house

Table of Contents

Warm Up with the Ganada Song

Before we dive into learning Hangeul-the Korean alphabets, let's start with a K-pop song called "Ganada Song" designed for you!

This song is similar to the ABC song. They attach the vowel "a" to consonants and sing "Ga, Na, Da, Ra, Ma, Ba, Sa, A, Ja, Cha, Ka, Ta, Pa, Ha"!

Shall we try? Sing along!

Ga, Na, Da, Ra, Ma, Ba, Sa, A, Ja, Cha, Ka, Ta, Pa, Ha.

가나다라마바사아자차카타파하

Now, let's listen to the Ga, Na, Da song.

Ganada Song

After listening to the song several times, try to sing along with the help of the romanized letters!

가 나 다 라 마 바 사 아 자 차 카 타 파 하
[ga na da ra ma ba sa a ja cha ka ta pa ha]

빠 람 빠 람 Let's sing along
[ppa ram ppa ram Let's sing along]

가 나 다 라 마 바 사 아 자 차 카 타 파 하
[ga na da ra ma ba sa a ja cha ka ta pa ha]

빠 람 빠 람 singing together

[ppa ram ppa ram singing together]

Let's walk and sing / Let's hold hands together

아 야 어 여 오 요 우 유 으 이

[a ya eo yeo o yo u yu eu i]

가.슴 을 펴 고

[ga. seum eul pyeo go]

나.를 따 라 해 봐

[na. reul tta ra hae bwa]

다.함 께

[da. ham kke]

라.라 라

[ra. ra ra]

마.음 열 고

[ma. eum yeol go]

바.라 봐

[ba. ra bwa]

사.이 좋 게

[sa. i jok ge]

아.름 답 게 Oh~

[a. reum dap ge Oh~]

자. 따 라 해 봐

[ja. tta ra hae bwa]

차. 렷. 하 나 둘 셋

[cha. ryeot ha na dul set]

카.네 이 션

[ka. ne i syeon]

타.고 서

[ta. go seo]

파.란 하 늘

[pa. ran ha neul]

보 고 웃 어 봐

[bo go us eo bwa]

하 하 하 하

[ha ha ha ha]

하! 하! 하!

[ha! ha! ha!]

가 나 다 라 마 바 사 아 자 차 카 타 파 하

[ga na da ra ma ba sa a ja cha ka ta pa ha]

빠 람 빠 람 Let's sing along

[ppa ram ppa ram Let's sing along]

가 나 다 라 마 바 사 아 자 차 카 타 파 하

[ga na da ra ma ba sa a ja cha ka ta pa ha]

빠 람 빠 람 singing together

[ppa ram ppa ram singing together]

Let's walk and sing / Let's hold hands together

아 야 어 여 오 요 우 유 으 이

[a ya eo yeo o yo u yu eu i]

We're together / Together is better / Me and You, we're one

Melodies are shared like a dream! / Languages Our look, Oh!

All isn't the same / Many differences

Let's sing me and you / Melody makes us one, together!

Singing brings peace and love

가 나 다 라 마 바 사 아 자 차 카 타 파 하

[ga na da ra ma ba sa a ja cha ka ta pa ha]

우 리 에 게 꿈 을 주 는 글

[u ri e ge kkum eul ju neun geul]

가 나 다 라 마 바 사 아 자 차 카 타 파 하
[ga na da ra ma ba sa a ja cha ka ta pa ha]

Born to give us hope and the dream

Let's walk and sing / Let's hold hands together

아 야 어 여 오 요 우 유 으 이
[a ya eo yeo o yo u yu eu i]

Let's go!

With this K-pop song, are you ready to embark on your journey with Hangeul?

K-팝과 함께 노래와 함께, 한글 여정을 시작할
준비가 되셨나요?

Let's go!

자, 함께 떠나봅시다!

What is Hangeul?

Now, you are going to read a conversation between your friends. Make sure to remember the information shared by the Jina Ssaem (쌤, teacher). You'll need to take a mini quiz at the end of your learning—see if you can get baek-jeom-man-jeom (백점만점)—full marks!

이제 여러분은 친구들 간의 대화를 읽게 됩니다. 지나쌤이 공유한 정보를 꼭 기억하세요!
학습을 마친 후 미니 퀴즈를 풀게 될 텐데요 — 백점만점(100점 만점)을 받을 수 있는지 확인해 보세요!

Sarang

Hello! Annyeonghaseyo! I have been dreaming of moving to Korea for years, and I'm finally going! My first step is to learn to read Korean. Join me and my friends as we learn about Hangeul!

안녕하세요! (안녕하세요!) 오래전부터 한국에 오고 싶었는데 드디어 오게 되었네요! 첫 번째 단계는 한글을 읽는 법을 배우는 것입니다.
저와 제 친구들과 함께 한글에 대해 배워보세요!

Jina Ssaem

Annyeonghaseyo! I'll do my best to help you along the way! I'm excited for your Korean journey to start.

안녕하세요! 여러분의 한국어 학습을 위해 최선을 다해 돕겠습니다.
여러분의 한국어 학습 여정이 시작되는 것이 정말 기대됩니다.

Sarang o———————————————

So, **WHAT** is Hangeul?

그렇다면, 한글이란 무엇일까요?

Jina Ssaem o———————————————

Hangeul(한글) is the Korean phonetic alphabet.
You can mix and match these characters to make up to
11,172 unique syllables, all of which can be easily sounded
out.
When Hangeul was created, it was said that you can learn
it in anywhere from one morning to 10 days, even if you're
not a genius.
Hangeul is simple and logical, making it quick and easy to
pick up.

한글은 한국어의 음소 문자입니다.
이 문자들을 조합하면 최대 11,172개의 고유한 음절을 만들 수 있으며,
모두 쉽게 발음할 수 있습니다. 한글이 창제되었을 때. 천재가 아니더라도
열흘 안에 배울 수 있다고 전해졌습니다. 한글은 단순하고 논리적이어서
빠르고 쉽게 배울 수 있습니다.

Priya o————————————————————

Okay, so **WHO** made Hangeul?

좋아요, 그렇다면 누가 한글을 만들었을까요?

Jina Ssaem □————————————————

King Sejong(세종 대왕) was a brilliant king in Korean history.

With help from a team of scholars, he personally created Hangeul.

King Sejong wrote about making Hangeul.

Here's a simple version of what he said:

세종대왕님은 한국 역사에서 매우 뛰어난 왕이었습니다. 학자들의 도움을 받아 한글을 직접 창제하셨습니다. 세종대왕님은 한글을 창제한 것에 대해 이렇게 말씀하셨습니다. 다음은 그 말씀을 간단히 정리한 내용입니다:

"This month, I made the 28 letters of Hangeul. These letters are based on old scripts and are divided into beginning, middle, and end sounds. When combined, they form syllables. The letters are simple yet versatile. They are called the 'Correct Sounds for the People.'"

"이번 달에 나는 한글 28자를 만들었다. 이 글자들은 고대 문자에 기반을 두고 있으며, 초성, 중성, 종성으로 나뉜다. 이 글자들을 조합하면 음절이 형성된다. 글자는 단순하면서도 활용도가 높다. 이 글자는 '백성을 위한 바른 소리'라고 불린다."

King Sejong wanted a writing system that was easy for everyone to learn, so more people could read and write in Korean.

세종대왕님은 모든 사람이 쉽게 배울 수 있는 문자 체계를 원하셨고, 이를 통해 더 많은 사람들이 한국어로 읽고 쓸 수 있기를 바라셨습니다.

Haru ○————————————————————

WHEN did King Sejong create Hangeul?

그렇다면 세종대왕님이 한글을 창제한 때는 언제인가요?

Jina Ssaem ○————————————————

The Korean language as it's spoken today has been around
for thousands of years. But Hangeul was completed in
late December of 1443 and officially promulgated by King
Sejong in 1446. It is one of the youngest writing systems
in the world!

오늘날 사용되는 한국어는 수천 년 동안 이어져 왔습니다. 하지만 한글은
1443년 12월 말에 완성되었고, 1446년에 세종대왕님에 의해 공식적으로
반포되었습니다. 한글은 세계에서 가장 젊은 문자 체계 중 하나입니다!

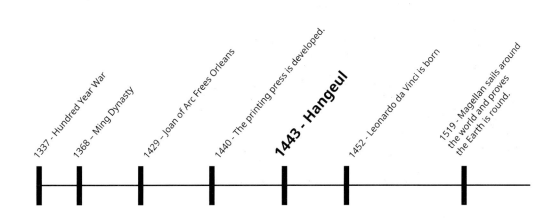

1337 - Hundred Year War | 1368 - Ming Dynasty | 1429 – Joan of Arc Frees Orleans | 1440 - The printing press is developed. | **1443 - Hangeul** | 1452 - Leonardo da Vinci is born | 1519 - Magellan sails around the world and proves the Earth is round.

Yu Tao ○————————————————————

WHERE did Hangeul come from?

그렇다면 한글은 어디에서 유래되었나요?

Jina Ssaem ○————————————————

King Sejong was an early king in the Joseon Dynasty, which is the older name for modern day Korea. Hangeul is totally native to Korea

세종대왕님은 조선 왕조 초기의 왕으로, 조선은 오늘날 한국의 옛 이름입니다. 한글은 완전히 한국 고유의 문자 체계입니다.

Hunminjeongeum
Haeryebon

Sam ○———————————————————

Okay, but if the Korean language has been around so long, **WHY** was Hangeul introduced?

그렇군요. 그렇다면 한국사람들이 사용하는 언어가 오래전부터 존재해왔는데도 왜 한글이 도입되었을까요?

Jina Ssaem ▭———————————————

Before Hangeul was created, Korean people had to use Chinese characters to write things down. King Sejong himself wrote:

한글이 창제되기 전에는 한국 사람들이 무언가를 기록할 때 한자를 사용해야만 했습니다. 세종대왕님께서 직접 이렇게 말씀하셨습니다:

"The Korean language is different from Chinese, so it is hard to express Korean by using Chinese characters. Hence, many people having something to put into words are unable to express their feelings. To overcome such distressing circumstances, I have newly devised twenty-eight letters that everyone can learn with ease and use with convenience in daily life."

"한국어는 중국어와 다르기 때문에 한자를 사용하여 한국어를 표현하기가 어렵다. 따라서 하고 싶은 말을 글로 표현해야 하는 많은 사람들이 자신의 감정을 제대로 표현하지 못하고 있는 실정이다. 이런 어려운 상황을 극복하기 위해. 누구나 쉽게 배우고 일상생활에서 편리하게 사용할 수 있는 스물여덟 글자를 새로 만들었다."

The King's choice to help illiterate people, like women and lower classes, was not popular. Some nobles and powerful figures thought Korea should be trying to be more like China, and that lower classes didn't need literacy.

세종대왕님이 여성과 하층민 같은 문맹층을 돕기 위해 한글을 창제한 결정은 당시에 인기가 없었습니다. 일부 귀족들과 권력자들은 한국이 중국을 더 본받아야 한다고 생각했으며, 하층민에게는 문해력이 필요하지 않다고 여겼습니다.

Despite opposition, Hangeul flourished among ordinary people, fulfilling King Sejong's vision of a simple, easy-to-learn writing system for everyone.

이런 반대에도 불구하고 한글은 일반 백성들 사이에서 널리 퍼졌으며, 세종대왕님이 꿈꿨던 모든 사람을 위한 쉽고 간단한 문자 체계라는 비전을 실현시켰습니다.

Sophia ○────────────────────────────

I've never heard of someone inventing an alphabet! **HOW** did Sejong do that?

저는 누군가가 알파벳을 발명했다는 이야기는 들어본 적이 없는데요! 세종대왕님은 그것을 어떻게 해내셨을까요?

Jina Ssaem ○────────────────────────

King Sejong used advanced linguistic principles to design the shapes of his letters. Consonants were modeled after the shape the mouth makes in their production, and vowels were modeled after Daoist spiritual principles.

세종대왕님은 고급 언어학적 원리를 활용해 글자의 모양을 설계하셨습니다. 자음은 발음할 때 입의 모양을 본떠 만들었고, 모음은 도교의 영적 원리를 기반으로 설계되었습니다.

In the following, you can see how the different letters fit the shape the mouth makes when making their sounds! You can also see the Daoist meanings of the basic vowel shapes (Heaven, Earth, and Human).

다음은 각 글자가 소리를 낼 때 입의 모양과 어떻게 맞는지 볼 수 있습니다! 또한, 기본 모음의 형태에 담긴 도교적 의미(하늘, 땅, 사람)도 확인할 수 있습니다.

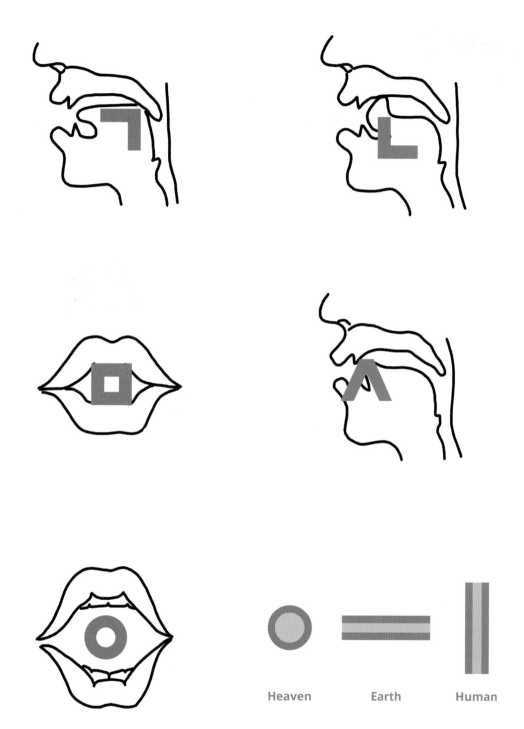

Heaven   Earth   Human

Sarang

Now that we've learned about Hangeul, I guess it's time to start learning!

이제 한글에 대해 배웠으니, 본격적으로 배우기 시작할 때가 된 것 같네요!

Jina Ssaem

Take a deep breath and take your time. You'll get this in no time!

깊게 숨을 들이쉬고 천천히 해보세요. 곧잘 해낼 수 있을 거예요!

Mini Quiz Your Path to Becoming a K-pop Idol through Hangeul!

한글 공부를 통해 K-pop 아이돌 되기!

Part 1. *Fill in the Blanks* 빈칸 채우기

Complete the sentences using the correct information from the conversation. Choose the correct answer from the options provided.

대화에서 제공된 정보를 사용하여 문장을 완성하세요. 보기 중에서 올바른 답을 선택하세요.

1. Hangeul is the Korean _____ alphabet.
   a) symbolic   b) phonetic   c) numerical

2. Hangeul was created by _____ with help from a team of scholars.
   a) King Sejong   b) Prince Yeonsan   c) Queen Seondeok

3. Before Hangeul, Korean people used _____ characters to write things down.
   a) Japanese   b) Mongolian   c) Chinese

4. The design of Hangeul letters is based on _____ principles.
   a) mathematical   b) linguistic   c) artistic

Part 2. *Matching* 연결하기

Match the information with the correct description. Draw lines to connect each term with its correct description.

용어에 대한 올바른 설명을 찾아 선으로 연결 하세요.

1. Hangeul   •   • a) Creator of Hangeul
2. King Sejong   •   • b) The year Hangeul was completed
3. 1443   •   • c) Where Hangeul originated
4. Joseon Dynasty   •   • d) The Korean phonetic alphabet
5. Chinese characters   •   • e) Used by Koreans before Hangeul was created

ANSWERS

Part 1. b a c b   *Part 2.* 1-d; 2-a; 3-b; 4-c; 5-e

Hangeul in Romanized Letters

First, let's talk about *romanized letters*-the way that Korean sounds are written in English letters.

먼저, 한국어 소리를 영어 알파벳으로 표기하는 방식인 로마자 표기에 대해 이야기해 봅시다.

Why is this important?

이것이 왜 중요할까요?

Romanized letters help you understand how to pronounce Korean words even if you can't read Hangeul yet. These are the official romanized letters used by the Korean government, so you will see them in names, places, and roman Korean words.

Sometimes, the way Korean words are spelled using English letters might seem a bit confusing or counterintuitive. Don't worry, you'll get the hang of it with practice!

로마자 표기는 한글을 아직 읽을 수 없어도 한국어 단어의 발음을 이해하는 데 도움이 됩니다. 이 표기는 한국 정부에서 공식적으로 사용하는 로마자 표기법이기 때문에 이름, 장소, 그리고 로마자로 표기된 한국어 단어에 서 자주 볼 수 있습니다. 가끔은 영어 알파벳으로 표기된 한국어 단어의 철자가 약간 혼란스럽거나 직관적이 지 않게 보일 수도 있습니다. 걱정하지 마세요, 연습하면 곧 익숙해질 거예요!

BASIC VOWELS
단모음

Now, let's look at the vowels. We will list the Korean characters and their romanized spelling. Refer back to the romanization chart if you need to review the pronunciation. Colour coding information: red is for heart on your side, blue is running underneath, purple is a mix of red and blue because it uses both ways, and green for consonants.

이제 모음에 대해 알아봅시다. 한국어 문자와 로마자로 표기한 스펠링을 나열할 예정입니다.
발음을 복습해야 한다면 로마자 표기표를 다시 참고하세요.

색상 코드 정보:
빨강: 심장이 있는 쪽 (왼쪽)
파랑: 아래쪽으로 흐름
보라: 빨강과 파랑의 혼합 (양쪽 방식을 사용)
초록: 자음을 나타냄

VOWEL	ROMANIZATION
ㅏ	*a*
ㅓ	*eo*
ㅗ	*o*
ㅜ	*u*
ㅡ	*eu*
ㅣ	*i*

아

Romanized Letter a

Hangeul ㅏ

English sound

ah as in f**a**ther or b**a**rk

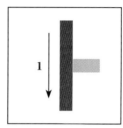 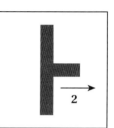

어

Romanized Letter eo

Hangeul ㅓ

English sound

uh as in f**u**n or s**o**n,
with more rounded lips

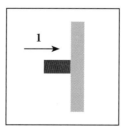 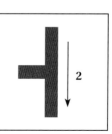

Romanized Letter   o

Hangeul   ㅗ

English sound

oh as in l**o**w or t**oe**

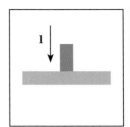 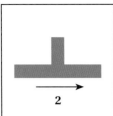

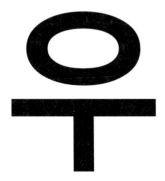

Romanized Letter   u

Hangeul   ㅜ

English sound

oo as in bl**ue** or t**oo**

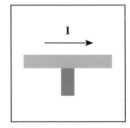 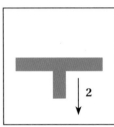

Romanized Letter   eu

Hangeul   —

English sound

eu as in f*oo*t or p*u*t

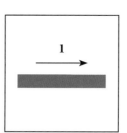

Romanized Letter   i

Hangeul   ㅣ

English sound

ee as in s*ee* or m*e*

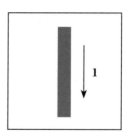

COMPLEX VOWELS
중모음

In addition to the simple vowel sounds we've already practiced, there are also more complex vowel sounds.

The first set of these complex vowel sounds are based on the basic vowels we have already learned. To make these vowels, we simply add a line (一) (|) to a basic vowel, which changes the vowel to start with a "y" sound.

우리가 이미 연습한 단순 모음 소리 외에도 더 복잡한 모음 소리가 있습니다. 이 복합 모음의 첫 번째 세트는 우리가 이미 배운 기본 모음을 바탕으로 합니다. 이 모음을 만들기 위해 기본 모음에 선(一) 또는 점(|)을 추가하면 모음이 "y" 소리로 시작하게 됩니다.

VOWEL	ROMANIZATION
ㅑ	*ya*
ㅕ	*yeo*
ㅛ	*yo*
ㅠ	*yu*
ㅒ	*ye*
ㅖ	*ye*

Romanized Letter   ya

Hangeul   ㅑ

English sound

ya as in **ya**rd

Romanized Letter   yeo

Hangeul   ㅕ

English sound

yuh as in **you**ng

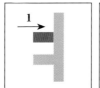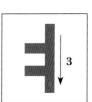

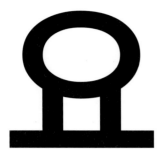

Romanized Letter   yo

Hangeul   ㅛ

English sound

yo as in ***yo***gurt
(American pronunciation)

Romanized Letter   yu

Hangeul   ㅠ

English sound

yoo as in ***you***

애

Romanized Letter	yae
Hangeul	ㅒ
English sound	
	yeh as in **ya**y

Romanized Letter	ye
Hangeul	ㅖ
English sound	
	yeh as in **ya**y

  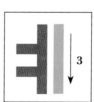

Try to write the following words:

ㅑ

야구 *Baseball* .... [yagu]

야채 *Vegetable* .... [yachae]

ㅕ

여자 *Woman* .... [yeoja]

여권 *Passport* .... [yeogwon]

ㅛ

요리 *Cooking* .... [yori]

요거트 *Yogurt* .... [yogeoteu]

ㅠ

유리 *Glass* .... [yuri]

유자차 *Citron tea* .... [yujacha]

ㅒ

얘기책 *Storybook* .... [yaegichaek]

얘들아 *Hey kids* .... [yaedeura]

ㅖ

예쁘다 *Pretty* .... [yeppeuda]

예약 *Reservation* .... [yeyak]

The next set of complex vowels are *diphthongs*, which means they are made by combining two other vowel sounds.

다음 복합 모음 세트는 "이중모음"으로, 두 개의 다른 모음 소리를 결합하여 만들어집니다.

COMBINATION	DIPHTHONG	ROMANIZATION
ㅏ + ㅣ	ㅐ	*ae*
ㅓ + ㅣ	ㅔ	*e*
ㅗ + ㅏ	ㅘ	*wa*
ㅗ + ㅐ	ㅙ	*wae*
ㅗ + ㅣ	ㅚ	*oe*
ㅜ + ㅓ	ㅝ	*wo*
ㅜ + ㅔ	ㅞ	*we*
ㅜ + ㅣ	ㅟ	*wi*
ㅡ + ㅣ	ㅢ	*ui*

애

Romanized Letter   ae

Hangeul   ㅐ

English sound
eh as in t*a*ke or ch*a*se

에

Romanized Letter   e

Hangeul   ㅔ

English sound
eh as in b*e*d or d*ea*d

와

Romanized Letter	wa
Hangeul	과
English sound	
	wah as in **wi**se

왜

Romanized Letter	wae
Hangeul	괘
English sound	
	weh as in **wa**it or **we**ight

  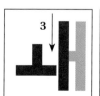 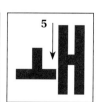

외

Romanized Letter oe

Hangeul ㅚ

English sound
weh as in **wa**it or **we**ight

워

Romanized Letter wo

Hangeul ㅝ

English sound

wo as in **wa**llet

   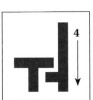

Romanized Letter   we

Hangeul   ㅞ

English sound
  weh as in **wa**it or **we**ight

Romanized Letter   wi

Hangeul   ㅟ

English sound
  we as in **wea**ve or **wee**d

Romanized Letter ui

Hangeul ㅢ

English sound
a combination of *eu*
and *i* above

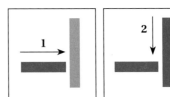

Try to write the following words:

다음 단어들을 한글로 써보세요:

ㅐ

개미 *Ant* .... [gaemi]

사랑해 *I love you* .... [saranghae]

ㅔ

메뉴 *Menu* .... [menyu]

케이크 *Cake* .... [keikeu]

과

과일 *Fruit* .... [gwail]

과자 *Snack* .... [gwaja]

ㅙ

왜 *Why* .... [wae]

돼지 *Pig* .... [dwaeji]

ㅚ

외국 *Foreign country* .... [oeguk]

회사 *Company* .... [hoesa]

ㅝ

원하다 *To want* .... [wonhada]

원숭이 *Monkey* .... [wonsungi]

ㅞ	웨이터 *Waiter*	[weiteo]
	웹사이트 *Website*	[wepsaiteu]

ㅟ	위험 *Danger*	[wiheom]
	위 *Up/Above*	[wi]

ㅢ	의사 *Doctor*	[uisa]
	의자 *Chair*	[uija]

Just like the basic vowels we already covered, each of these vowels combines with various consonants to create different syllable sounds. Below are some examples of those combinations.

기본 모음에서 배운 것처럼, 이 모음들도 또한 다양한 자음과 결합하여 서로 다른 음절 소리를 만듭니다. 아래는 이러한 결합의 몇 가지 예입니다.

바	*bya*		뮈	*mwi*
겨	*gyeo*		붜	*bwo*
료	*ryo*		갸	*gya*
뮤	*myu*		뢔	*rwae*
대	*dae*		뇨	*nyo*
얘	*yae*		새	*sae*
네	*ne*		뒈	*dwe*

혜	*hye*		유	*yu*
콰	*kwa*		죠	*jyo*
푀	*poe*		혀	*hyeo*
쇄	*swae*		냬	*nyae*
퉈	*two*		킈	*kui*
줴	*jwe*		체	*che*

Try To Write The Following Words:

비행기 *Airplane* .... [bihaenggi]

겨울 *Winter* .... [gyeoul]

뮤지컬 *Musical* .... [myujikeol]

돼지 *Pig* .... [dwaeji]

사랑해 *I love you* .... [saranghae]

유자차 *Citron tea* .... [yujacha]

BASIC CONSONANTS

자음

Romanized Letter   g

Hangeul   ㄱ

English sound
a softer version (unvoiced)
of *g* as in *g*ood

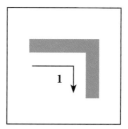

Romanized Letter   n

Hangeul   ㄴ

English sound
n as in *n*ame

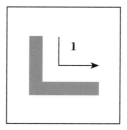

Romanized Letter   d

Hangeul   ㄷ

English sound
a softer version (unvoiced) of *d* as
in *d*awn

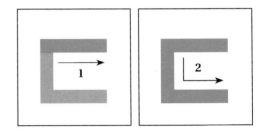

Romanized Letter   r

Hangeul   ㄹ

English sound
a *r* that involves rolling and
vibrating the tongue

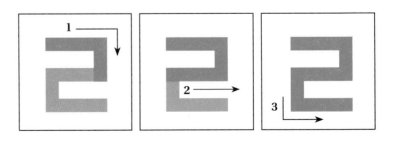

Romanized Letter   m

Hangeul   ㅁ

English sound

m as in ***m***ask

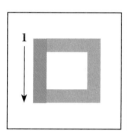 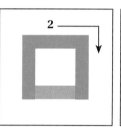 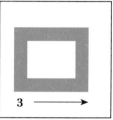

Romanized Letter   b

Hangeul   ㅂ

English sound
a softer version (unvoiced) of *b* as
in ***b***all

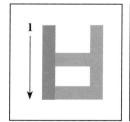 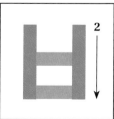 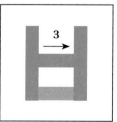 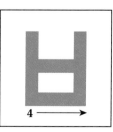

Romanized Letter   S

Hangeul   ㅅ

English sound

                                        s as in **s**ad

 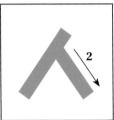

Romanized Letter   ng

Hangeul   ㅇ

English sound

                                   ng as in so**ng**
                              (at the end of a word)

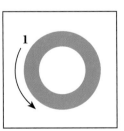

Romanized Letter   j

Hangeul   ㅈ

English sound

a softer version
(unvoiced) of *j* as in *j*et

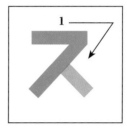 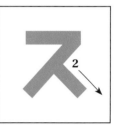

ASPIRATED CONSONANTS
격음

Romanized Letter	ch
Hangeul	ㅊ
English sound	
	ch as in ***ch***art

 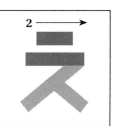  

Romanized Letter	k
Hangeul	ㅋ
English sound	
	k as in ***k***id

 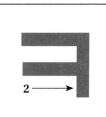

Romanized Letter   t

Hangeul   ㅌ

English sound

t as in *t*all

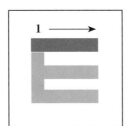  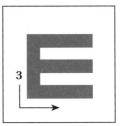

Romanized Letter   p

Hangeul   ㅍ

English sound

p as in *p*aper

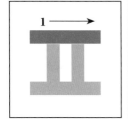 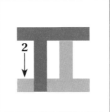 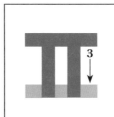 

Romanized Letter	h
Hangeul	ㅎ
English sound	
	h as in *h*ow or *h*ot

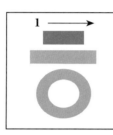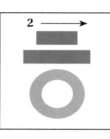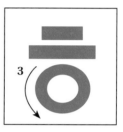

REINFORCED CONSONANTS
경음

In addition to these aspirated consonants, Korean also has several *reinforced* consonants. These are formed by doubling other consonant sounds by closing up the throat, to make a harder, more forceful sound.

격음 외에도, 한국어에는 여러 강화된 자음(된소리)이 있습니다. 이 자음들은 다른 자음 소리를 두 번 반복하거나 목을 더 조여서 더 강하고 단단한 소리를 내는 방식으로 형성됩니다.

Romanized Letter	kk
Hangeul	ㄲ
English sound	
	a tenser *g* than the *g* in *g*ood

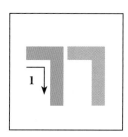 

Romanized Letter	tt
Hangeul	ㄸ
English sound	
	a tenser *d* than the *d* in *d*og

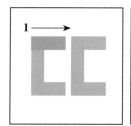 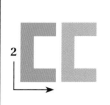 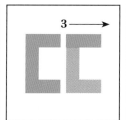 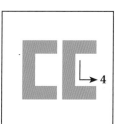

Romanized Letter　　　　　　pp

Hangeul　　　　　　　　　　ㅃ

English sound

a tenser *b* than
the *b* in **b**all

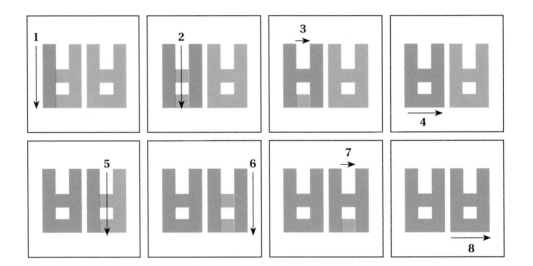

Romanized Letter　　　　　ss

Hangeul　　　　　ㅆ

English sound
　　a tenser *s* than the *s* in **s**ad

  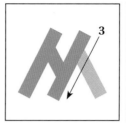 

Romanized Letter　　　　　jj

Hangeul　　　　　ㅉ

English sound
　　a tenser *j* than the *j* in **j**et

Romanized Letter	Hangeul	English sound
a	ㅏ	*ah* as in f*a*ther or b*a*rk
eo	ㅓ	*uh* as in f*u*n or s*o*n, with more rounded lips
o	ㅗ	*oh* as in l*o*w or t*oe*
u	ㅜ	*oo* as in bl*ue* or t*oo*
eu	ㅡ	*eu* as in f*oo*t or p*u*t
i	ㅣ	*ee* as in s*ee* or m*e*
ae	ㅐ	*eh* as in t*a*ke or ch*a*se
e	ㅔ	*eh* as in b*e*d or d*ea*d
wa	ㅘ	*wah* as in *wi*se
wae	ㅙ	*weh* as in w*a*it or *we*ight
oe	ㅚ	*weh* as in w*a*it or *we*ight
wo	ㅝ	*wo* as in *wa*llet
we	ㅞ	*weh* as in w*a*it or *we*ight
wi	ㅟ	*we* as in *wea*ve or *wee*d
ui	ㅢ	a combination of *eu* and *i* above
ya	ㅑ	*ya* as in *ya*rd
yeo	ㅕ	*yuh* as in *you*ng
yo	ㅛ	*yo* as in *yo*gurt (American pronunciation)
yu	ㅠ	*yoo* as in *you*
yae	ㅒ	*yeh* as in *ya*y

Romanized Letter	Hangeul	English sound
ye	ㅖ	*yeh* as in **ya**y
g	ㄱ	a softer version (unvoiced) of g as in **g**ood
n	ㄴ	*n* as in **n**ame
d	ㄷ	a softer version (unvoiced) of *d* as in **d**awn
r	ㄹ	a *r* that involves rolling and vibrating the tongue
m	ㅁ	m as in **m**ask
b	ㅂ	a softer version (unvoiced) of *b* as in **b**all
s	ㅅ	*s* as in **s**ad
ng	ㅇ	n*g* as in so**ng** (at the end of a word)
j	ㅈ	a softer version (unvoiced) of *j* as in **j**et
ch	ㅊ	*ch* as in **ch**art
k	ㅋ	*k* as in **k**id
t	ㅌ	*t* as in **t**all
p	ㅍ	*p* as in **p**aper
h	ㅎ	*h* as in **h**ow or **h**ot
kk	ㄲ	a tenser *g* than the *g* in **g**ood
tt	ㄸ	a tenser *d* than the *d* in **d**og
pp	ㅃ	a tenser *b* than the *b* in **b**all
ss	ㅆ	a tenser *s* than the *s* in **s**ad
jj	ㅉ	a tenser *j* than the *j* in **j**et

How to Make a Hangeul Block

Do you still remember our Ganada Song?
Let's play some games!

우리의 "가나다 송"을 아직 기억하고 있나요? 그렇다면 게임을 시작해 봅시다.

Mini Quiz Can you try to fill out the missing words for our song!
노래의 빈칸을 채워볼까요! 준비되셨다면 시작해 보세요!

가	_ㅏ	다	라	마	바	_ㅏ
_a	na	da	_a	ma	_a	sa
아	자	_ㅏ	카	_ㅏ	파	_ㅏ
a	ja	cha	_a	ta	pa	ha

아	야	어	여	오	요	우
a	ya	eo	yeo	o	yo	u
유	으	이				
yu	eu	i				

ANSWERS

g ㄴ r b ㅅ ㅊ k ㅌ ㅎ

74

Let's look at the Ganada song again. Can you identify and circle the combinations with just one consonant and one vowel?

"가나다 송"을 다시 살펴봅시다. 자음 하나와 모음 하나로 이루어진 조합을 찾아보고 동그라미로 표시해 보세요!

가나다라마바사아자차카타파하
빠람빠람 Let's sing along

가나다라마바사아자차카타파하
빠람빠람 singing together

Let's walk and sing
Let's hold hands together
아야어여오요우유으이

가.슴을 펴고
나.를 따라해봐
다.함께
라.라라
마.음 열고
바.라봐
사.이좋게
아.름답게 Oh~
자.따라해봐
차.렷.하나둘셋
카.네이션
타.고서
파.란하늘
보고 웃어봐
하하하하
하!하!하!

가나다라마바사아자차카타파하
빠람빠람 Let's sing along

가나다라마바사아자차카타파하
빠람빠람 singing together

Let's walk and sing
Let's hold hands together
아야어여오요우유으이

We're together
Together is better
Me and You, we're one
Melodies are shared like a dream! Languages Our look, Oh!
All isn't the same / Many differences
Let's sing me and you / Melody makes us one, together!
Singing brings peace and love

가나다라마바사아자차카타파하
우리에게 꿈을 주는 글
가나다라마바사아자차카타파하
Born to give us hope and the dream

Let's walk and sing
Let's hold hands together
아야어여오요우유으이
Let's go !

C_1	V_2

These are syllable cluster shapes that put the vowel (i.e., side vowels) to the right side of the first consonant. The letters are sounded out in the order represented by the numbers in the boxes (1, 2, 3 etc.).

이 음절 구조는 모음(즉, 옆에 위치하는 모음)을 첫 번째 자음의 오른쪽에 배치합니다. 글자는 상자 안의 숫자(1, 2, 3 등) 순서대로 발음됩니다.

C_1	V_2
C_3	

C_1	V_2
C_3	C_4

다

Look at these examples of the combinations listed above.

위에서 설명한 조합의 예를 살펴보세요.

달	닭

These are syllable cluster shapes that put the vowel underneath the first consonant (i.e.,bottom vowels). The letters are sounded out in the order represented by the numbers in the boxes.

이 음절 구조는 모음을 첫 번째 자음의 아래에 배치합니다(즉, 아래에 위치하는 모음). 글자는 상자 안에 표시된 숫자 순서대로 발음됩니다.

C_1

V_2

C_1

V_2

C_3

C_1

V_2

C_3 C_4

Look at these examples of the combinations listed above.

위에서 설명한 조합의 예를 살펴보세요.

모

목

몫

Let's look at the combination of consonants with vowels. The vowels ㅏ, ㅓ, and ㅣ attach to the side of the consonant, and the vowels ㅗ, ㅜ, and ㅡ attach to the bottom of the consonant. Make sure to look back at the romanization chart to check pronunciation!

자음과 모음의 결합을 살펴봅시다. 모음 **ㅏ, ㅓ, ㅣ**는 자음의 **옆**에 붙고, 모음 **ㅗ, ㅜ, ㅡ**는 자음의 **아래**에 붙습니다. 발음을 확인하려면 로마자 표기표를 다시 참고하세요!

Try to write the following words: 다음 단어들을 한글로 써보세요:

ㅏ	가지마 *Don't go*	[gajima]
	가족 *Family*	[gajok]
ㅓ	저 *I*	[jeo]
	처음 *First time*	[cheoeum]
ㅗ	노래 *Song*	[norae]
	조금 *A little*	[jogeum]
ㅜ	누나 *Older sister*	[nuna]
	후루룩 *Slurping sound*	[hurureuk]
ㅣ	다시 *Again*	[dashi]
	미소 *Smile*	[miso]

ㄱ

ㄱ + ㅏ 가 *ga*	ㄱ + ㅗ 고 *go*
ㄱ + ㅓ 거 *geo*	ㄱ + ㅜ 구 *gu*
ㄱ + ㅣ 기 *gi*	ㄱ + ㅡ 그 *geu*

Try to write the following words:

고기 *Meat* [gogi]

고	기						

가게 *Shop* [gage]

가	게						

기차 *Train* [gicha]

기	차						

ㄴ

ㄴ + ㅏ 나 *na*	ㄴ + ㅗ 노 *no*
ㄴ + ㅓ 너 *neo*	ㄴ + ㅜ 누 *nu*
ㄴ + ㅣ 니 *ni*	ㄴ + ㅡ 느 *neu*

Try to write the following words:

누나 *Older sister* [nuna]

누	나						

나이 *Age* [nai]

나	이						

노래 *Song* [norae]

노	래						

Fun Fact

In Korean, "**nuna**" is used by males to address an older sister or female, "**oppa**" by females for an older brother or male, "**eonni**" by females for an older sister or female, and "**hyung**" by males for an older brother or male.

한국어에서 "누나"는 남성이 본인보다 나이가 많은 여성을 부를 때 사용합니다. "오빠"는 여성이 본인보다 나이가 많은 남성을 부를 때 사용합니다. "언니"는 여성이 본인보다 나이가 많은 여성을 부를 때 사용합니다. "형"은 남성이 본인보다 나이가 많은 남성을 부를 때 사용합니다.

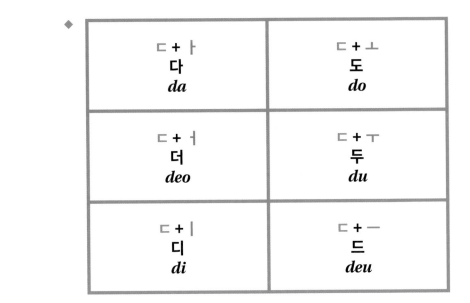

ㄷ

ㄷ + ㅏ 다 *da*	ㄷ + ㅗ 도 *do*
ㄷ + ㅓ 더 *deo*	ㄷ + ㅜ 두 *du*
ㄷ + ㅣ 디 *di*	ㄷ + ㅡ 드 *deu*

Try to write the following words:

다시 *Again* [dashi]

다	시					

두부 김치 *Tofu kimchi* [dubukimchi]

두	부	김	치			

더 많이 *More* [deo mani]

더	많	이			

다음 *Next* [daeum]

다	음					

ㄹ

◆

ㄹ + ㅏ **라** *ra*	ㄹ + ㅗ **로** *ro*
ㄹ + ㅓ **러** *reo*	ㄹ + ㅜ **루** *ru*
ㄹ + ㅣ **리** *ri*	ㄹ + ㅡ **르** *reu*

Try to write the following words:

라면 *Ramen* [ramyeon]

라	면						

리조트 *Resort* [rijoteu]

리	조	트			

로션 *Lotion* [rosyeon]

로	션						

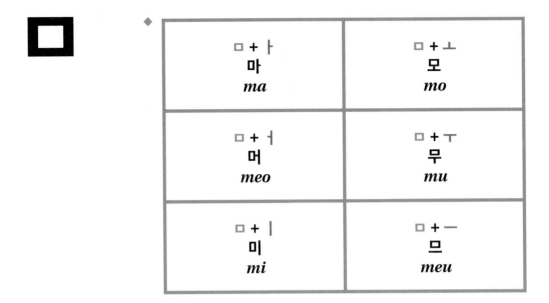

ㅁ + ㅏ 마 *ma*	ㅁ + ㅗ 모 *mo*
ㅁ + ㅓ 머 *meo*	ㅁ + ㅜ 무 *mu*
ㅁ + ㅣ 미 *mi*	ㅁ + ㅡ 므 *meu*

Try to write the following words:

마음 *Heart* [maeum]

마	음						

미소 *Smile* [miso]

미	소						

메뉴 *Menu* [menyu]

메	뉴						

ㅂ

ㅂ + ㅏ **바** *ba*	ㅂ + ㅗ **보** *bo*
ㅂ + ㅓ **버** *beo*	ㅂ + ㅜ **부** *bu*
ㅂ + ㅣ **비** *bi*	ㅂ + ㅡ **브** *beu*

Try to write the following words:

밥 *Rice* [bap]

밥							

바다 *Sea* [bada]

바	다						

비행기 *Airplane* [bihaenggi]

비	행	기			

버스 *Bus* [beoseu]

버	스					

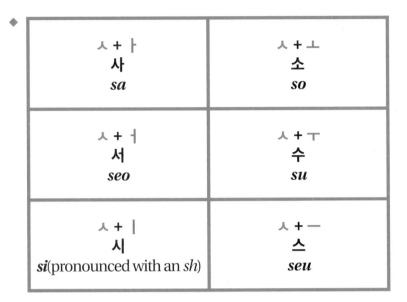

Try to write the following words:

사랑해 *I love you* [saranghae]

사	랑	해			

수능 *Korean college entrance exam* [suneung]

수	능					

소리 *Sound* [sori]

소	리					

식당 *Restaurant* [sikdang]

식	당					

Fun Fact

Suneung is Korea's national college entrance exam, similar to the SAT. It's crucial for university admission and influences students' futures significantly.

"수능"은 한국의 대학교 입학 시험으로, 미국의 SAT와 유사합니다. 이는 대학 입학에 필수적이며 학생들의 미래에 큰 영향을 미칩니다.

ㅇ + ㅏ **아** *a*	ㅇ + ㅗ **오** *o*
ㅇ + ㅓ **어** *eo*	ㅇ + ㅜ **우** *u*
ㅇ + ㅣ **이** *i*	ㅇ + ㅡ **으** *eu*

At the beginning
of syllables, this
consonant is silent.

음절의 처음에 위치할 때,
이 자음은 소리가 나지 않습니다.

Try to write the following words:

우리 *We/Us* [uri]

아빠 *Dad* [appa]

영어 *English* [yeongeo]

오늘 *Today* [oneul]

ㅈ

ㅈ + ㅏ **자** *ja*	ㅈ + ㅗ **조** *jo*
ㅈ + ㅓ **저** *jeo*	ㅈ + ㅜ **주** *ju*
ㅈ + ㅣ **지** *ji*	ㅈ + ㅡ **즈** *jeu*

Try to write the following words:

저 *I* [jeo]

저							

조금 *A little* [jogeum]

조	금						

잡채 *Japchae* [japchae]

잡	채						

지하철 *Subway* [jihacheol]

지	하	철			

ㅊ + ㅏ **차** *cha*	ㅊ + ㅗ **초** *cho*
ㅊ + ㅓ **처** *cheo*	ㅊ + ㅜ **추** *chu*
ㅊ + ㅣ **치** *chi*	ㅊ + ㅡ **츠** *cheu*

The aspirated
version of ㅈ

ㅈ의 격음 버전은 ㅊ 입니다.

Try to write the following words:

차 *Car* [cha]

차							

처음 *First time* [cheoeum]

처	음					

친구 *Friend* [chingu]

친	구					

초과 근무 *Overtime* [chogwa geunmu]

초	과	근	무			

Fun Fact

Overtime work is a significant issue in Korea. Many employees work long hours, often beyond their official workday, which can lead to stress, burnout, and work-life imbalance.

초과근무는 한국에서 중요한 문제입니다. 많은 직원들이 공식 근무 시간을 넘어 장시간 일하는 경우가 많아 스트레스, 번아웃, 그리고 일과 삶의 균형 상실로 이어질 수 있습니다.

ㅋ

ㅋ + ㅏ **카** ***ka***	ㅋ + ㅗ **코** ***ko***
ㅋ + ㅓ **커** ***keo***	ㅋ + ㅜ **쿠** ***ku***
ㅋ + ㅣ **키** ***ki***	ㅋ + ㅡ **크** ***keu***

The aspirated
version of ㄱ

ㄱ의 격음 버전은 ㅋ 입니다.

Try to write the following words:

커피 *Coffee* [keopi]

콜라 *Cola* [kolla]

코트 *Coat* [koteu]

컴퓨터 *Computer* [keompyuteo]

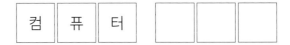

ㅌ ◆

ㅌ + ㅏ **타** *ta*	ㅌ + ㅗ **토** *to*
ㅌ + ㅓ **터** *teo*	ㅌ + ㅜ **투** *tu*
ㅌ + ㅣ **티** *ti*	ㅌ + ㅡ **트** *teu*

The aspirated
version of ㄷ

ㄷ의 격음 버전은 ㅌ입니다.

Try to write the following words:

토마토 *Tomato* [tomato]

티켓 *Ticket* [tiket]

택시 *Taxi* [taeksi]

토너 *Toner* [toneo]

ㅍ + ㅏ **파** *pa*	ㅍ + ㅗ **포** *po*
ㅍ + ㅓ **퍼** *peo*	ㅍ + ㅜ **푸** *pu*
ㅍ + ㅣ **피** *pi*	ㅍ + ㅡ **프** *peu*

The aspirated
version of ㅂ

ㅂ의 격음 버전은 ㅍ 입니다.

Try to write the following words:

파티 *Party* [pati]

파	티					

푸른 *Blue / Green* [pureun]

푸	른					

프라이머 *Primer* [peuraimeo]

프	라	이	머			

표 *Ticket* [pyo]

표						

Fun Fact

Pureun can describe both "blue" and "green". Historically, the language didn't differentiate between these two colors as distinctly as in English. Instead, 푸른 refers to a broad spectrum of cool colors that include both blue and green, especially when describing nature, like the sky or the grass.

"푸른"은 "파란"과 "초록"을 모두 표현할 수 있는 말입니다. 예전부터 한국어에서는 이 두 색을 영어처럼 명확히 구분하지 않았으며, 대신 푸른색은 하늘이나 풀처럼 자연을 묘사할 때 사용되며 넓은 범위의 차가운 색을 포함합니다.

ㅎ + ㅏ 하 *ha*	ㅎ + ㅗ 호 *ho*
ㅎ + ㅓ 허 *heo*	ㅎ + ㅜ 후 *hu*
ㅎ + ㅣ 히 *hi*	ㅎ + ㅡ 흐 *heu*

The aspirated
version of ㅇ

ㅇ의 격음 버전은 ㅎ 입니다.

Try to write the following words:

행복 *Happiness* [haengbok]

행	복						

하늘 *Sky* [haneul]

하	늘						

호텔 *Hotel* [hotel]

호	텔						

화장실 *Restroom* [hwajangsil]

화	장	실			

ㄲ

ㄲ + ㅏ **까** *kka*	ㄲ + ㅗ **꼬** *kko*
ㄲ + ㅓ **꺼** *kkeo*	ㄲ + ㅜ **꾸** *kku*
ㄲ + ㅣ **끼** *kki*	ㄲ + ㅡ **끄** *kkeu*

The reinforced
version of ㄱ

ㄱ의 된소리(강화된) 버전은 ㄲ 입니다.

Try to write the following words:

꼬마 *Kid* [kkoma]

꼬	마						

끄다 *To turn off* [kkeuda]

끄	다						

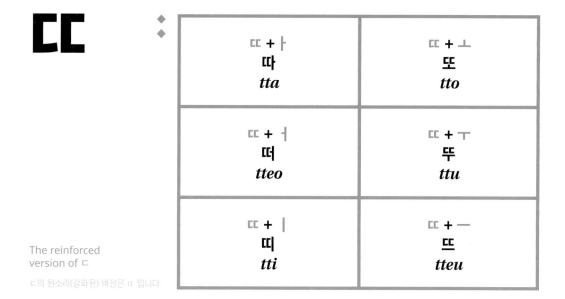

The reinforced
version of ㄷ

ㄷ의 된소리(강화된) 버전은 ㄸ 입니다.

Try to write the following words:

또 *Again* [tto]

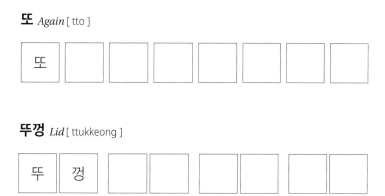

뚜껑 *Lid* [ttukkeong]

◆
◆

ㅃ + ㅏ **빠** *ppa*	ㅃ + ㅗ **뽀** *ppo*
ㅃ + ㅓ **뻐** *ppeo*	ㅃ + ㅜ **뿌** *ppu*
ㅃ + ㅣ **삐** *ppi*	ㅃ + ㅡ **쁘** *ppeu*

The reinforced
version of ㅂ (p)

ㅂ의 된소리(강화된) 버전은 ㅃ 입니다.

Try to write the following words:

뽀로로 *Pororo* [ppororo]

뽀	로	로			

쁘띠 *Petite* [ppeutti]

쁘	띠						

ㅆ + ㅏ **싸** *ssa*	ㅆ + ㅗ **쏘** *sso*
ㅆ + ㅓ **써** *sseo*	ㅆ + ㅜ **쑤** *ssu*
ㅆ + ㅣ **씨** **ssi** (pronounced as *sh*)	ㅆ + ㅡ **쓰** *sseu*

The reinforced
version of ㅅ

ㅅ의 된소리(강화된) 버전은 ㅆ 입니다.

Try to write the following words:

싸가지 *Rude* [ssagaji]

싸	가	지			

쓰다 *To write/use* [sseuda]

쓰	다						

ㅉ + ㅏ 짜 *jja*	ㅉ + ㅗ 쪼 *jjo*
ㅉ + ㅓ 쩌 *jjeo*	ㅉ + ㅜ 쭈 *jju*
ㅉ + ㅣ 찌 *jji*	ㅉ + ㅡ 쯔 *jjeu*

The reinforced
version of ㅈ

ㅈ의 된소리(강화된) 버전은 ㅉ 입니다.

Try to write the following words:

짜장면 *Jjajangmyeon* [jjajangmyeon]

짜	장	면			

짬뽕 *Jjamppong* [jjamppong]

짬	뽕						

Chapter 05

Consonants
at the Bottom
[Batchim]

CONSONANTS
AT THE END OF SYLLABLES

받침: 음절의 끝에 오는 자음

When the consonant comes at the end of the syllable, it always sits at the bottom, whether the vowel is a "side" vowel or a "bottom" vowel. The consonant sound at the end of the syllable is different from the consonant sound at the beginning of the syllable. The following are examples of each consonant at the end of a syllable.

자음이 음절의 끝에 올 때는, 모음이 "옆 모음"이든 "아래 모음"이든 항상 아래쪽에 위치합니다. 음절 끝에 오는 자음 소리는 음절의 처음에 오는 자음 소리와 다르게 발음됩니다. 다음은 음절 끝에 각 자음이 오는 예시들입니다.

At the end of a syllable, ㄱ makes a soft *k* sound by closing up the throat, as in loc***k*** or ca***k***e.

ㄱ: 목을 조이며 부드러운 k 소리를 냅니다. (예: lock, cake)

약　　[yak]　　**medicine**
죽　　[juk]　　**porridge**

Try to write the following words:

식당 *Restaurant* [sikdang]

....

음악 *Music* [eumak]

....

한국 *Korea* [hanguk]

....

ㄴ

At the end of a syllable, ㄴ makes an *n* sound, as in ru**n** or ma**n**. It is the same sound as when it appears in the beginning.

ㄴ: n 소리를 냅니다. (예: run, man) 이는 처음에 나타날 때와 같은 소리입니다.

선 [seon] **line**
분 [bun] **person**

Try to write the following words:

은행 *Bank* [eunhaeng]

사진 *Photo* [sajin]

신분증 *ID Card* [sinbunjeung]

관광지 *Tourist attraction* [gwangwangji]

At the end of a syllable, ㄷ makes a soft *t* sound by closing up the throat, as in ha**t** or ho**t**.

ㄷ: 목을 조이며 부드러운 t 소리를 냅니다. (예: hat, hot)

받	[bat]	**to receive (받다 *batda*)**
곧	[got]	**soon**

Try to write the following words:

받다 *Receive* [batda]

....

믿다 *Believe* [mitda]

....

At the end of a syllable, ㄹ makes an *l* sound, as in ha**ll** or sma**ll**.

ㄹ: l 소리를 냅니다. (예: hall, small)

| 털 | [teol] | **fur** |
| 굴 | [gul] | **cave** |

Try to write the following words:

월요일 *Monday* [woryoil]

....

호텔 *Hotel* [hotel]

....

불고기 *Grilled meat* [bulgogi]

....

서울 *Seoul* [seoul]

....

갈비탕 *Beef rib soup* [galbitang]

....

At the end of a syllable, ㅁ makes an *m* sound, as in hi**m** or ja**m**. It is the same sound as when it appears in the beginning.

ㅁ: m 소리를 냅니다. (예: him, jam) 이는 처음에 나타날 때와 같은 소리입니다.

잠	[jam]	**sleep**
봄	[bom]	**spring**

Try to write the following words:

감자탕 *Pork bone soup* [gamjatang]

....

짐 *Luggage* [jim]

....

음식 *Food* [eumsik]

....

ㅂ

At the end of a syllable, ㅂ makes a soft *p* sound by closing up the throat, as in sla**p** or to**p**.

ㅂ: 목을 조이며 부드러운 p 소리를 냅니다. (예: slap, top)

집   [jip]   **house**

즙   [jeup]   **juice**

Try to write the following words:

김밥 *Seaweed rice rolls* [gimbap]

....

잡채 *Stir-fried glass noodles* [japchae]

....

밥 *Rice* [bap]

....

At the end of a syllable, ㅅ makes a soft *t* sound by closing up the throat , as in ha*t* or ho*t*.

ㅅ: 목을 조여 부드러운 t 소리를 냅니다. (예: hat, hot.)

것   [geot]   **thing**
곳   [got]   **place**

Try to write the following words:

맛 *Taste* [mat]

....

옷 *Clothes* [ot]

....

낫 *Sickle* [nat]

....

At the end of a syllable, ㅇ makes an *ng* sound, as in so**ng** or thi**ng**.

ㅇ: ng 소리를 냅니다. (예: song, thing.)

| 방 | [bang] | **room** |
| 등 | [deung] | **lantern, light** |

Try to write the following words:

공항 *Airport* [gonghang]

....

중앙 *Center* [jungang]

....

성공 *Success* [seonggong]

....

영어 *English* [yeongeo]

....

ㅈ

At the end of a syllable, ㅈ makes a soft *t* sound by closing up the throat, as in ha***t*** or ho***t***.

ㅈ: 목을 조여 부드러운 t 소리를 냅니다. (예: hat, hot.)

낮 [nat] **afternoon**

늦 [got] **late** (늦다 *neutda*)

Try to write the following words:

맞아! *Correct!* [maja]

곶감 *Dried persimmon* [gotgam]

ㅊ

At the end of a syllable, ㅊ makes a soft *t* sound by closing up the throat, as in ha*t* or ho*t*.

ㅊ: 목을 조여 부드러운 t 소리를 냅니다. (예: hat, hot.)

빛	[bit]	**light**
꽃	[ggot]	**flower**

Try to write the following words:

윷놀이 *A traditional board game* [yutnori]

....

꽃병 *Vase* [kkotbyeong]

....

Fun Fact

Yutnori is a traditional Korean board game played with four wooden sticks called 윷 (yut). Players or teams throw the sticks to move markers around a board, aiming to complete a circuit before the opponent. It's popular during holidays like Lunar New Year.

윷놀이(Yutnori)는 네 개의 나무막대인 윷을 사용하여 즐기는 한국의 전통 보드게임입니다. 플레이어나 팀이 윷을 던져 말을 움직이며, 상대보다 먼저 한 바퀴를 완주하는 것이 목표입니다. 특히 설날과 같은 명절에 많이 즐겨지는 놀이입니다.

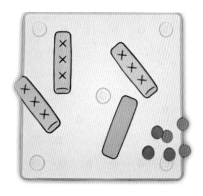

ㅋ

At the end of a syllable, ㅋ makes a soft *k* sound by closing up the throat, as in loc**k** or ca**ke**.

ㅋ: 목을 조여 부드러운 k 소리를 냅니다. (예: lock, cake.)

억   [eok]   **kitchen (부엌 *bueok*)**

읔   [euk]   **the ㅋ letter (키읔 *kieuk*)**

Try to write the following words:

부엌 *kitchen* [bueok]

At the end of a syllable, ㅌ makes a soft *t* sound, as in hat or hot. You won't actually pronounce the t—rather let your tongue stop before letting the *t* sound out. Take a look at the following two examples:

ㅌ: 부드러운 t 소리를 냅니다. 그러나 실제로 t 소리를 완전히 발음하지 않고 혀가 멈추게 합니다. (예: hat, hot.)

밑   [mit]   **underneath**

붙   [but]   **to attach (붙다 *butda*)**

Try to write the following words:

뱉다 *To spit* [baetda]

....

맡다 *To smell/sniff* [matda]

....

113

ㅍ

At the end of a syllable, ㅍ makes a *p* sound by closing up the throat, as in sla**p** or to**p**.

ㅍ: 목을 조여 p 소리를 냅니다. (예: slap, top.)

잎   [ip]   **leaf**

높   [nop]   **high (높다 *nopda*)**

Try to write the following words:

숲 *Forest* [sup]

앞 *Front* [ap]

덮다 *To cover* [deopda]

At the end of a syllable, ㅎ makes a soft aspirated *t* sound, as in ha*t* or ho*t* with some puffs of air.

ㅎ: 약간의 공기를 동반한 부드러운 t 소리를 냅니다. (예: hat, hot.)

닿   [nat]   **to touch** (닿다 *data*)

놓   [not]   **to put/set (something) down** (놓다 *nota*)

Try to write the following words:

좋다 *Good* [jota]

....

놓다 *To put* [nota]

....

115

ᄁ **❖❖** ....

At the end of a syllable, ㄲ makes a soft *k* sound by closing up the throat, as in lo**ck** or ca**k**e.

ㄲ: 목을 조여 부드러운 k 소리를 냅니다. (예: lock, cake.)

닦   [dakk]   **to wipe clean (닦다 *dakkda*)**

묶   [mukk]   **to tie (묶다 *mukkda*)**

Try to write the following words:

밖에 *Outside* [bakke]

....

At the end of a syllable, ㅆ makes a soft *t* sound by closing up the throat, as in ha*t* or ho*t*.

ㅆ: 목을 조여 부드러운 t 소리를 냅니다. (예: hat, hot.)

었   [eot]   **commonly found in past tense**

ㅆ doesn't usually appear as a final letter with ㅗ, ㅜ, or ㅡ vowels.
ㄸ , ㅃ , and ㅉ don't usually appear at the end of a syllable.

Try to write the following words:

있다 *To exist* [itda]

....

맛있다 *Delicious* [masitda]

....

Consonant clusters often appear at the end of Korean words, following the batchim pronunciation rules. These clusters simplify into seven core sounds: ㄱ, ㄴ, ㄷ, ㄹ, ㅁ, ㅂ, and ㅇ, especially before another consonant or at the word's end. The table below shows examples of how these clusters are simplified.

한국어 단어의 끝부분에서는 자주 자음군이 나타나며, 이는 받침 발음 규칙을 따릅니다. 이러한 자음 군은 특히 다른 자음 앞이나 단어의 끝에서 다음의 7가지 핵심 소리로 단순화됩니다: ㄱ, ㄴ, ㄷ, ㄹ, ㅁ, ㅂ, ㅇ. 아래 표는 이러한 자음 군이 어떻게 단순화되는지 보여줍니다.

WORD	ROMANIZATION	PRONOUNCE
닭	dalk	*dak*
밟	balp	*bap*
읽	ilk	*ik*
붉	bulk	*buk*
꿇	ggult	*ggul*
값	gapt	*gap*
옳	olt	*ol*
엀	eont	*eon*
읊	eulp	*eup*

What is the name of your favourite K-pop band?

당신이 가장 좋아하는 K-pop 밴드의 이름은 무엇인가요?

What is the name of your favourite K-pop song?

당신이 가장 좋아하는 K-pop 노래의 제목은 무엇인가요?

What is the name of your BIAS?

당신이 가장 좋아하는 멤버(BIAS)의 이름은 무엇인가요?

Now, pick your favourite K-pop song or any Korean song. Can you try to find more words that have double consonants at the bottom? Write them down here:

이제, 좋아하는 K-pop이나 한국 노래를 하나 선택해 보세요. 그 노래의 가사에서 받침에 쌍자음이 포함된 단어들을 찾아볼 수 있나요? 찾은 단어들을 여기에 적어보세요:

Putting It All Together

Many words in Korean are formed by putting together multiple syllables. Sometimes, the ending of one syllable will affect the pronunciation at the beginning of the next syllable. The following are examples of some of these syllable combinations.

한국어에서 많은 단어는 여러 음절을 결합하여 형성됩니다. 때로는 한 음절의 끝 소리가 다음 음절의 처음 소리에 영향을 미치기도 합니다. 다음은 이러한 음절 조합의 예시들입니다.

Sound Change Rule 1

When one syllable is following by another syllable that begins with the silent consonant ㅇ, the sound from the first syllable carries over. Look at the example:

한 음절 뒤에 ㅇ으로 시작하는 음절이 올 경우, 첫 번째 음절의 소리가 다음 음절로 이어집니다. 예를 살펴보세요:

먹어요 to eat　　➡　　머거요 *meogeoyo*

받아요 to receive　　➡　　바다요 *badayo*

달아요 to be sweet　➡　　다라요 *darayo*

The spelling doesn't change–but the pronunciation does!

Try to pronounce these words!

읽어요 To read　　⋯▸　　[일거요] *ilgeoyo*

앉아요 To sit　　⋯▸　　[안자요] *anjayo*

좋아요 To be good　⋯▸　　[조아요] *joayo*

Sound Change Rule 2

Some letters change pronunciation when followed or preceded by a nasal consonant (ㄴ, ㅁ, ㅇ). Look at the following examples to find patterns:

코와 비강음화: 자음이 비음(ㄴ, ㅁ, ㅇ) 앞뒤에서 소리가 바뀌는 경우

한국어에서는 특정 자음이 비음(코소리 자음)인 ㄴ, ㅁ, ㅇ 앞뒤에 위치할 때 발음이 변화합니다. 아래 예시를 통해 패턴을 살펴보세요:

합니다 to do	➡	함니다 *hamnida*
국물 broth	➡	궁물 *gungmul*
정리 arrangement	➡	정니 *jeongni*
ㅂ + ㄴ / ㅁ / ㅇ	➡	ㅁ + ㄴ / ㅁ / ㅇ
ㄱ + ㄴ / ㅁ / ㅇ	➡	ㅇ + ㄴ / ㅁ / ㅇ
ㄴ / ㅁ / ㅇ + ㄹ	➡	ㄴ / ㅁ / ㅇ + ㄴ

There are more examples of this rule, so keep a look out!

Try to pronounce these words!

독립 Independence	⋯➤	[동닙]	*dongnip*
박물관 Museum	⋯➤	[방물관]	*bangmulgwan*
작년 Last year	⋯➤	[장년]	*jangnyeon*

Sound Change Rule 3

~~~~~~

When two ㄹ characters appear next to each other, they make an l sound. When ㄴ appears next to ㄹ, ㄴ also changes to ㄹ. Look at the following examples:

ㄹ 음운 규칙: 두 개의 ㄹ과 ㄴ+ㄹ 조합의 발음 변화 한국어에서는 다음과 같은 발음 변화 규칙이 적용됩니다:

연락 contact through message or call
➡ 	열락 *yeollak*

전라도 Jeolla Province
➡ 	절라도 *jeollado*

난로 stove ➡ 날로 *nallo*

ㄹ + ㄹ ➡ ㄹ + ㄹ

ㄴ + ㄹ ➡ ㄹ + ㄹ

Remember that only the pronunciation, not the spelling, changes!

Try to pronounce these words!

설날 Lunar New Year

⋯▸   [설랄] *seollal*

신라 Name of an ancient Korean kingdom

⋯▸   [실라] *silla*

한라산 Name of a famous mountain in Korea

⋯▸   [할라산] *hallasan*

Fun Fact

Seollal is the Korean Lunar New Year, a major holiday celebrating the first day of the lunar calendar. Families gather to perform ancestral rites, eat traditional foods like tteokguk (rice cake soup), and play games like 윷놀이. It's a time for honoring ancestors and spending time with family.

재미있는 사실 **설날**은 음력 설로, 음력 새해 첫날을 축하하는 한국의 중요한 명절입니다. 가족들이 모여 차례와 같은 전통적인 제사를 지내고, 떡국(떡국)과 같은 전통 음식을 먹으며, 윷놀이 같은 게임을 즐깁니다. 이날은 조상을 기리고 가족과 함께 시간을 보내는 특별한 날입니다.

Sound Change Rule 4

When ㄷ or ㅌ is followed by 이 or 히, they change to ㅈ or ㅊ respectively. Look at the following examples:

ㄷ/ㅌ 음운 규칙: 이 또는 히와 결합 시 발음 변화

한국어에서는 ㄷ이나 ㅌ이 이 또는 히 뒤에 올 경우, 각각 ㅈ 또는 ㅊ으로 바뀌어 발음됩니다.

맏이 eldest child	➡	**마지** *maji*
닫혀요 to be closed	➡	**다쳐요** *dachyeoyo*
같이 together	➡	**가치** *gachi*

ㄷ + ㅇ	➡	**ㅈ**
ㄷ + ㅎ	➡	**ㅊ**
ㅌ + ㅇ/ㅎ	➡	**ㅊ**

While the pronunciation changes, the spelling remains the same.

Try to pronounce these words!

굳이 Insistently	⋯⟶	**[구지]** *guji*
갇히다 To be locked up	⋯⟶	**[가치다]** *gachida*
밭이 Field	⋯⟶	**[바치]** *bachi*

LET'S TRY TO READ SOME COMMON WORDS!

사람	*Person*		집	*House*
물	*Water*		밥	*Rice / Meal*
책	*Book*		차	*Car / Tea*
나무	*Tree*		고양이	*Cat*
개	*Dog*		꽃	*Flower*
문	*Door*		공	*Ball*
손	*Hand*		눈	*Eye / Snow*
산	*Mountain*		시간	*Time*
하늘	*Sky*		얼굴	*Face*

K-FOOD CHALLENGE

Take 30 seconds to think about your top 3 K-food. Draw them on the space provided. Then, look for how they are written in Korean!

30초 동안 당신이 가장 좋아하는 K-food 3가지를 생각해 보세요. 빈 칸에 그림으로 표현해 보세요. 그런 다음, 그 음식들의 이름을 한국어로 적어 보세요.

Essential Korean Expressions and Fun K-Words

안녕하세요	Hello
반갑습니다	Nice to meet you
안녕히 계세요	Goodbye [you're leaving]
저는 [NAME] 입니다	My name is ____
감사합니다	Thank you
괜찮아요	It's fine/No problem
잠시만요	Excuse me [getting someone's attention]
네	Yes
아니요	No
미안해요	Sorry
어디에서 오셨어요?	Where are you from?
영어 할 수 있으세요?	Do you speak English?
이해가 되지 않아요	I don't understand
[NOUN] 있어요?	Is there ____?/Do you have ____?

[NOUN] 어디예요?	Where is ____?
이게 뭐예요?	What is this?
얼마예요?	How much is it?
이거 주세요	Please can I have this/I want this
도와주세요	Please help me
잘 먹겠습니다	Thank you for the meal [before eating]
잘 먹었습니다	Thank you for the meal [after eating]
맛있어요	It's delicious
카드로 지불해도 될까요?	Can I pay by card?
봉투를 주시겠어요?	Can I get a bag?
너무 비쌉니다	It's too expensive

K-POP WORDS

앨범 *Album*

빌보드 *Billboard*

보이그룹 *Boy group*

안무 *Choreography*

컴백 *Comeback*

작곡가 *Composer*

콘서트 *Concert*

댄스팀 *Dance team*

데뷔 *Debut*

눈 *Eyes*

팬 *Fan*

팬덤 *Fandom*

팬미팅 *Fan meeting*

이별 *Farewell/Breakup*

걸그룹 *Girl group*

손 *Hand*

행복 *Happiness*

가슴 *Heart/Chest*

마음 *Heart/Mind*

나 *I/Me*

아이돌 *Idol*

그룹 *K-pop group*

리더 *Leader*

레전드 *Legend*

그리움 *Longing/Nostalgia*

사랑 *Love*

메인보컬 *Main vocal*

멤버 *Member*

기억 *Memory*

뮤비 *MV*

뮤비촬영 *MV shooting*

이제 *Now*

오에스티 *Original soundtrack*

공연 *Performance*

연습실 *Practice room*

홍보 *Promotion*

랩 *Rap*

랩라인 *Rap line*

가수 *Singer*

미소 *Smile*

노래 *Song*

소리 *Sound*

목소리 *Voice*

무대 *Stage*

서브보컬 *Sub vocal*

K-POP WORDS

눈물 *Tears*

그때 *Then/At that time*

시간 *Time*

연습생 *Trainee*

트레이너 *Trainer*

함께 *Together*

예능 *Variety show*

보컬 *Vocal*

브이로그 *Vlog*

기다림 *Waiting*

너 *You*

그대 *You (formal)*

K-BEAUTY WORDS

액세서리 *Accessory*

미용 *Beauty*

브랜드 *Brand*

캐주얼 *Casual*

클렌징 *Cleansing*

의상 *Clothing*

컬렉션 *Collection*

코디 *Coordination*

화장품 *Cosmetics*

뷰티크리에이터 *Beauty creator*

블러셔 *Blusher*

디자이너 *Designer*

드레스 *Dress*

아이라이너 *Eyeliner*

패션 *Fashion*

의상디자인 *Fashion design*

패션아이콘 *Fashion icon*

패션쇼 *Fashion show*

포멀 *Formal*

파운데이션 *Foundation*

헤어컷 *Haircut*

립스틱 *Lipstick*

로션 *Lotion*

명품 *Luxury*

메이크업 *Makeup*

마스카라 *Mascara*

모델 *Model*

수분크림 *Moisturizer*

미용실 *Salon*

세럼 *Serum*

셔츠 *Shirt*

쇼핑 *Shopping*

피부관리 *Skin care*

스타일 *Style*

스타일링 *Styling*

스타일리스트 *Stylist*

트렌드 *Trend*

토너 *Toner*

K-TRAVEL ──────────────────

숙소 *Accommodation*

비행기 *Airplane*

공항 *Airport*

북촌한옥마을 *Bukchon Hanok Village*

버스 *Bus*

창덕궁 *Changdeokgung Palace*

경복궁 *Gyeongbokgung Palace*

한강공원 *Hangang Park*

호텔 *Hotel*

인사동 *Insadong*

제주도 *Jeju Island*

여행가방 *Luggage*

지도 *Map*

남산서울타워 *Namsan Seoul Tower*

여권 *Passport*

비행기표 *Plane ticket*

렌터카 *Rental car*

예약 *Reservation*

관광객 *Tourist*

관광명소 *Tourist attraction*

여행 *Travel*

여행사 *Travel agency*

여행일정 *Travel itinerary*

기차 *Train*

관광 *Sightseeing*

지하철 *Subway*

비자 *Visa*

K-DRAMA WORDS

액션 *Action*

배우 *Actor*

여배우 *Actress*

연기 *Acting*

오디션 *Audition*

방송 *Broadcast*

방송국 *Broadcasting Station*

캐릭터 *Character*

코미디 *Comedy*

드라마 *Drama*

감독 *Director*

촬영 *Filming*

주인공 *Main character*

멜로 *Melodrama*

프로듀서 *Producer*

리메이크 *Remake*

로맨스 *Romance*

시즌 *Season*

대본 *Script*

조연 *Supporting role*

K-WORK

상사 *Boss*

경력 *Career*

회사 *Company*

출근 *Commute*

동료 *Colleague*

직원 *Employee*

직업 *Job*

퇴근 *Leave the office*

회의 *Meeting*

신입사원 *New employee*

프로젝트 *Project*

승진 *Promotion*

채용 *Recruitment*

월급 *Salary*

업무 *Task*

팀워크 *Teamwork*

휴가 *Vacation*

일 *Work*

근무시간 *Working hours*

직장 *Workplace*

K-FOOD

비빔밥 *Bibimbap (mixed rice with vegetables and meat)*

소고기 *Beef*

불고기 *Bulgogi (marinated beef)*

닭고기 *Chicken*

냉면 *Cold noodles*

생선 *Fish*

음식 *Food*

과일 *Fruit*

김밥 *Gimbap (Korean rice roll)*

김치 *Kimchi*

고기 *Meat*

돼지고기 *Pork*

밥 *Rice/Meal*

떡 *Rice cake*

해산물 *Seafood*

반찬 *Side dishes*

국 *Soup*

간장 *Soy sauce*

찌개 *Stew*

야채 *Vegetables*

Congratulations! You've learned Hangeul!

축하합니다! 여러분은 한글을 완전히 익혔습니다!

You've reached the end of your **Annyeong? Hangeul!** journey.
안녕? 한글! 여정을 끝까지 완수하셨습니다.

From mastering the basic consonants and vowels to forming your very first words, you've taken big steps in learning the Korean language. We hope you had as much fun learning and practicing as we did guiding you through each step of the journey.
기본 자음과 모음을 배우고, 마침내 여러분의 첫 단어를 만들기까지, 한국어 학습에서 큰 도약을 이루셨습니다. 우리가 이 학습 과정을 함께하며 즐거움을 느꼈듯이, 여러분들도 학습과 연습을 즐기셨기를 바랍니다.

But remember, this is just the beginning! There's a whole world of Korean language and culture waiting for you to explore.
하지만 기억하세요, 이것은 시작일 뿐입니다! 한국어와 한국 문화의 넓은 세계가 여러분을 기다리고 있습니다.

In the next book, we'll dive deeper into Korean grammar, expressions, and more exciting language tips.
다음 책에서는 한국어 문법, 표현, 그리고 더 흥미로운 언어 팁들을 더 깊이 탐구할 예정입니다.

Thank you for joining us on this adventure. We can't wait to see you in the next book, where we'll continue this amazing journey together.
이 모험에 함께해 주셔서 감사합니다. 다음 책에서 다시 만날 날을 고대하며, 함께 이 놀라운 여정을 계속해 나가길 기대합니다.

Until then, 안녕히 계세요!

안녕? 한글!

초판인쇄 2025년 01월 24일
초판발행 2025년 01월 24일

지은이 조지은, 데릭 드릭스, 김형석
펴낸이 허대우
마케팅 김철규 / 황현경
편집 및 디자인 브런치파크
표지 디자인 이승미
캐릭터 디자인 이재엽
Special Support by 이종인

펴낸곳 주식회사 헬로우코리안
주소 경기도 고양시 덕양구 향동로217, 10층 KA1014호
문의 hello@hellokorean.co.kr
출판신고 2024년 6월 28일 제395-2024-000141호
인쇄 헬로우프린텍

ISBN 979-11-988638-4-3 13700